LOSING GROUND

DONOVAN WYLIE

Afterword by Andrew O'Hagan

FOURTH ESTATE · LONDON

1993–1995, Gloucestershire

1995–1997, Whitechapel, Bethnal Green, Seven Sisters

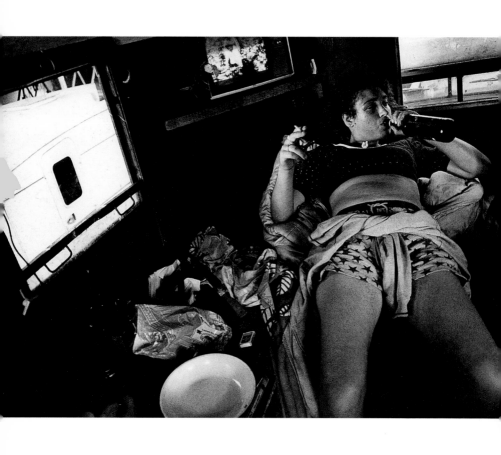

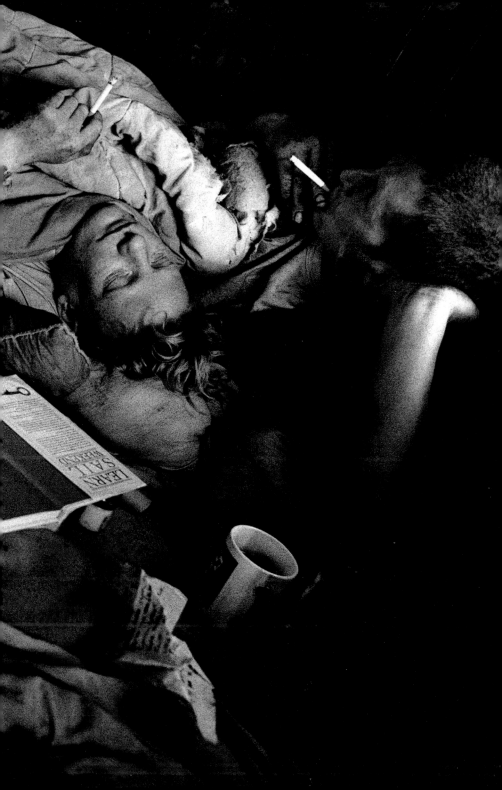

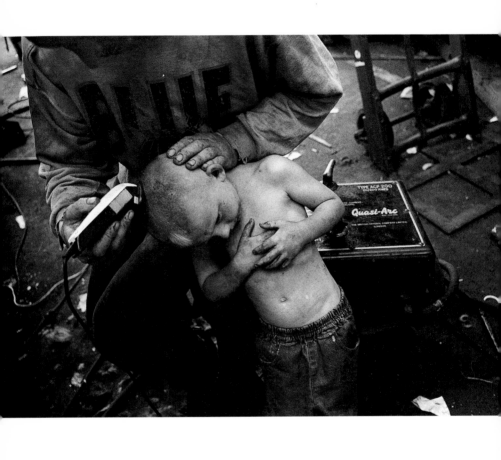

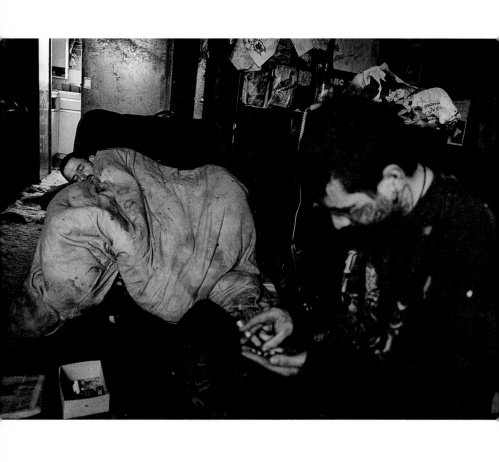

THESE PICTURES put me in mind of a certain father and son. The father was a bit older than photography, and the son was about the same age. Thomas Annan was born in 1829 and is remembered, by some more than others, for the work of his later years, when he first used his camera to record urban poverty. Annan's *Old Closes and Streets of Glasgow* was a shocker in its day. The pictures changed the way that many Britons understood themselves, and those ghostly shapes, those horrible tenements, those crooked and dirty children, lay long in the minds of the following day's Improvers. James Craig Annan was his father's image, but his own pictures are different. The best ones, *The Beach at Zandvoort* and *On a Dutch Shore*, are fairly rare-seeming disclosures: small people crowding to the shore front; a struggle there to survive against ocean and wind – against forces, moreover, quite invisible in the scene itself. You could say that where old Annan was a raiser of conscience, his dreamy son was a raiser of consciousness. But each possessed something of the other's talent.

Donovan Wylie has a bit of each Annan too. In the first place he is interested in the conditions of people's lives. He came to adulthood during the 1980s, a time when Britain showed, as it had shown before, how deeply it could fall in love with its own viciousness. Where the late Victorians spoke of the 'undeserving poor', the new Victorians, the Thatcherites, spoke of 'no such thing as society'. Both phrases must be among the most chilling ever used by elected leaders in the name of prosperity. Margaret Thatcher could seem all of a Herod in her heyday, someone almost cartoonishly cruel, a true hater of vulnerability. Even at this distance, with newer Herodians carrying on her business, it is impossible to forget her own cold handling of a country she hardly knew. And in truth few of us knew it. The Britain of the last twenty years has been a vastly under-described territory.

I remember seeing Thomas Annan's pictures a hundred years on. They were on display in the People's Palace, in a Glasgow that had travelled far from the horrors he described, and then travelled some way back. I wondered then – in two senses – who would show the return. In the years since then I haven't seen much that truly captured the circumstances of those new, dilapidated lives. Few had followed them with sufficient care, with ample heart, with a right degree of non-judgement, an open imagination and the blessings of a fine technique. Then I saw these pictures of Donovan Wylie's. He had himself taken an interest in those Eighties dispossessions, but in the new pictures he followed a thoroughly Nineties tribe, a group who left the society that did not exist, and who made a society for themselves, and then watched it die away. Wylie has come up with a photographic document in shape of a novel. I believe it is new to me, and new to itself. His book is an even distillation of social empathy and narrative control. He watches these sad lives sadly, and gives us a record of a way of life. His people are very much themselves in his photographs: he has caught them in the middle of a journey from an alternative life to no life at all. Wylie shows himself to be a formidable recording spirit, a scrupulous demon of the present tense. Here is a story we have not quite heard. A story of some modern lives lived at the outer edges: of society, of selfhood, of idealism, of oblivion. And the story is true.

Wylie is the youngest photographer ever to be accepted by Magnum. He was born in Belfast in 1971, to a Catholic mother and a Protestant father, and seems always to have had a feeling for exclusion, and self-exclusion too. In 1993 he found a large group of New Age travellers in a lay-by somewhere between Bath and Stroud. They were grouped together in old caravans and buses. He got speaking to one of the girls there – her name was Di – and he told her how he'd been thinking about poverty in Britain. 'There's no poverty here,' she said; 'this is paradise.' And the earlier pictures in this book do show a sort of paradise maintained. Children are held aloft, or run smiling past the camera; on a summer's day they play in a field with dogs, a piece of junk, a metal rotary blade, held to the sky like a beneficent sun. In the midst of these untidy lives there is at first a sense of order, a notion of provision, and we know that cakes are made, and music is played, and things are all right as they are.

Then something happens and the mood changes. Pushed out by the Criminal Justice Act, their choice of life no longer seems like a choice. They are taking drugs, and lying down, like a generation of the prematurely bedridden. They are necking bottles of vodka or shooting up. Some of them drifted off to the cities to beg, or to lose themselves, or something. A few others moved on to a site in London's Whitechapel, and it is there, over a year later, that Wylie picks up the story. The change is immense. No making, no interest in the land, no baking. The people at Whitechapel and Bethnal Green seem ill and hunted, their days given over to emptiness and boredom, the bottle, the needle. They stare off to nowhere. They eat from McDonald's cartons, draw signs saying 'Hungry'. They cower, oblivious, under rotten blankets, or sit in a dreary garage full of broken baths, the remnants of some other life, of cleanliness perhaps, or domestic pride. And all the time Wylie has no announcement to make about these people. They are simply there. And they are not-so-simply changed.

Where there is derangement, Wylie's eye arranges: where there is obviousness, he brings subtlety. In one of the pictures a small boy is crying in the snow. His head is leaning against the door of one of the buses; we see his crumpled face reflected in the cold metal. The snow covers the earth indiscriminately – crisp and even, as they say – and all of nature seems impervious to the private grief of this young boy with the scraggly hair. The picture seems to say something: snow falls wherever it falls, on no two lives the same, and it falls here, among this rubbish and decay, and here, as in many places, you will find a small boy crying against a door. And there in the distance, at the top of the frame, as if to guarantee this unkempt boy the chance of a place in the universality of childhood, there is a swing on a tree, there to take him up, as a laughing child, or leave him behind, to adult woes. The picture is simple and gracious and beautiful. Its grey shadows are everybody's.

I doubt if Donovan Wylie would be much interested, as I am, in the work of Annan and son. In the most important ways – ways quite personal, quite stylistic – they are a hundred miles apart, as well as a hundred years. The Annans were almost clinically impersonal. And the truth might be that the pictures in *Losing Ground* have as much to do with the condition of Donovan Wylie as they do with the conditions of underclass Britain. That is the sort of photographer he is. He works in the first person. And how surely do we feel the benefit of his human attachments. One of the girls who appears in this book stopped Wylie one day. 'The only reason we let you into our lives,' she said, 'is because you're just as vulnerable as us.'

So here they are. Donovan Wylie's own quiet songs of innocence and experience. Some make you angry and hopeless, a few make you disgusted and pitiless, some make you wonder what's to be done. But most of them just make you know more than you knew before. They show you something of the external world, and show it through internalising eyes. No one could think themselves the worse for that. With pictures like these you see how to see.

ANDREW O'HAGAN

First published in Great Britain in 1998 by
Fourth Estate Limited
6 Salem Road, London W2 4BU

Losing Ground is published simultaneously with an exhibition
at the National Museum of Photography, Bradford

A catalogue record for this book is available from
the British Library.

ISBN 1 85702 918 6

Printed in Great Britain by Butler & Tanner, London and Frome